HORRIBLE JOBS OF THE

RENAISSANCE

Gareth Stevens
Publishing

**LOUISE
SPILSBURY**

Please visit our website, www.garethstevens.com.
For a free color catalog of all our high-quality books,
call toll free 1-800-542-2595 or fax 1-877-542-2596.

Library of Congress Cataloging-in-Publication Data

Spilsbury, Louise.
Horrible jobs of the Renaissance / by Louise Spilsbury.
  p. cm. — (History's most horrible jobs)
Includes index.
ISBN 978-1-4824-0371-8 (pbk.)
ISBN 978-1-4824-0373-2 (6-pack)
ISBN 978-1-4824-0370-1 (library binding)
1. Renaissance — Juvenile literature. I. Spilsbury, Louise. II. Title.
CB353.S65 2014
940.2—dc23

First Edition

Published in 2014 by
Gareth Stevens Publishing
111 East 14th Street, Suite 349
New York, NY 10003

© 2014 Gareth Stevens Publishing

Produced by Calcium, www.calciumcreative.co.uk
Designed by Simon Borrough
Edited by Sarah Eason and Rachel Blount

Cover Illustration by Jim Mitchell

Photo credits: Dreamstime: 3drenderings 9b, Aigarsr 13, Alehnia 5b, Aprescindere 21, Bdingman 6, Bepsphoto 42c, Cammeraydave 38t, Chronicler 31t, Danace2000 36, Emprise 34, Epantha 42b, Georgios 39, Jdanne 17, Ksurrr 22, Matauw 32, Padmayogini 23, Photoshow 20l, 24, Toonerman 35r; Shutterstock: 38b, Natalia Bratslavsky 8, Paul Cowan 31b, Ermess 41t, Zack Frank 12, Oleg Golovnev 35l, Lineartestpilot 33b, Marcos81 4, Morphart Creation 18b, 33t, Luciano Mortula 26, NuConcept 25c, 25b, Pavila 40, Richcat 30, Kiev Victor 15b, Suttipon Yakham 20r; Wikipedia: 16, 25t, Giuseppe Bertini 44, Bibliothèque Nationale de France 37t, Galleria Borghese 45b, Paul A. Cziko 37b, Hans von Gersdorff 18c, Bartholomäus Bruyn the Elder 15t, Walker Art Gallery 11, Jebulon 7, Paul Lacroix 27, Lobsterthermidor 10, Yale Center for British Art 45t, Met Museum 29, OwenX 41b, Rowlandson Thomas 43, Esaias van de Velde 9t, The Yorck Project 19; www.aurorascarnival.co.uk: 14; www.fromoldbooks.org: 5t.

Printed in the United States of America.

CPSIA compliance information: Batch #CW14GS: For further information contact Gareth Stevens, New York, New York at 1-800-542-2595.

Contents

Chapter One
The Renaissance

Renaissance means rebirth in French. The Renaissance is also an important period in history. It started around 600 years ago, when huge changes in ideas and culture took place across Europe.

During the Renaissance the cathedral in Florence was given a huge dome, like those created by the Romans in ancient times.

New Ideas

The Renaissance began in the early fifteenth century when some scholars and artists in northern Italy started to study books discovered in ancient libraries. The books contained the ideas, art, and writings of people from ancient Greece and Rome. Studying the past inspired fresh ways of thinking. One of these was to experience and describe the world directly. This led to more voyages overseas in search of different cultures and riches. Another new idea was to trust in the leadership of wealthy citizens and not just church leaders.

Spreading Ideas

Ideas spread to Germany, Spain, and other countries over the following decades and centuries partly due to the invention of the printing press. This machine meant that books could be made much more quickly and more cheaply than when they had to be written by hand. With books more widely available, more people learned how to read. As a result, ideas spread faster. Even though the Renaissance was an exciting time of new ideas, there were still many horrible jobs to do.

The printing press provided people with a great variety of books.

New Art

Even today, Renaissance artists are some of the most famous names in art. These include Leonardo da Vinci and Michelangelo. They invented new ways of painting to make pictures appear more real. They developed perspective, which creates the illusion of depth in a two-dimensional image. They also started to draw from nature by studying the real proportions of the human body and not just imagining what it looked like.

David is a famous sculpture by the Italian Renaissance artist Michelangelo.

Life in the Cities

In the Renaissance, cities grew as they got wealthier. The richest people were kings and queens, leaders of regions called dukes, and merchants and bankers. They grew rich through taxes paid by the people and by trading in goods. For example, fine Italian cloth and weapons were exported and spices, gold, and other precious goods from countries such as America and China were imported.

A Great Divide

During the Renaissance, there was a great divide in wealth between the rich, who could afford luxuries, and the poor, who took manual jobs and served the rich. However, the poor at least now had the chance to become richer by working hard. Many people moved to cities, because there they found lots of jobs, even though some of those jobs were far from glamorous!

Elaborate, expensive clothing was used to display great wealth and status.

Smelly Fuller

Rich people in Renaissance times wore suits and gowns made from fine velvets, embroidered wool cloth, and expensive furs. When their clothes became dirty, the fine cloths could not be easily washed without damaging them. To deal with the problem, the rich employed a fuller. A fuller's job was to remove the grease from sheep's wool before it was woven into cloth. Fullers also cleaned people's clothes. They didn't use sweet-smelling soaps to remove stains from these luxurious clothes, however. Instead, fullers used a mixture of mud and old, smelly urine!

COSIMO PATER PATRIAE

Cosimo di Giovanni de' Medici, born in 1389, was the first of the Medici dynasty.

Richest Family?

The richest family in Renaissance Europe was probably the Medicis. They were merchants who created the first major bank in Florence, Italy. Family members, such as Cosimo, showed off their wealth by commissioning architects to create great private and public buildings. The Medicis also employed artists, such as Michelangelo, to sculpt and paint fine artworks to adorn the city's churches and other buildings.

Spit Boys

In the Renaissance, poor people did the worst jobs, and also ate the worst food. While the poor dined on a watery oatmeal called gruel, the rich ate roasted meats, such as mutton, beef, and even heron and swan. Most meat was roasted over an open fire. That is where spit boys earned their money.

By turning the spit, the spit boy made sure the meat cooked evenly.

Hot, Hot, Hot!

Spit boys turned long iron rods called spits onto which huge chunks of meat were skewered. It was the spit boys' job to roast the meat evenly. The meat was so heavy that only strong men, not boys, could turn it. "Spit boy" was simply the name used for the job. This job was one of the worst in Renaissance kitchens. The men had to sit close to a fire for hours on end, and were singed by the flames or splattered with hot fat.

At the Dining Table

Rich people ate lots of meat, but also ate other foods. They ate puddings made from cooked fruit, because they believed raw fruit was poisonous. Foreign treats brought back to Europe by explorers, such as corn and sweet potatoes, were popular, too. The rich ate lots of food with sweet, spicy flavors—they helped to mask the food's true, unpleasant taste! With no fridges to keep the food fresh, it often went bad.

The rich enjoyed elaborate feasts of roasted meats and birds, cooked by poor spit boys.

THE HORRIBLE TRUTH

In Renaissance times, city people would have thought you were crazy if you asked for a glass of water. Water came from rivers and wells, which were polluted. Most people drank wine or beer, because the process of making these drinks killed bugs that made the water unsafe to drink.

Gruesome Grooms

The wealthy Renaissance people had many servants to help them dress, to do their washing, to prepare their food, and to care for and educate their children. Some people even had servants who wiped their bottoms!

The King's Groom

King Henry VIII employed a groom of the stole (stool). The groom fetched the close stool, which was a box with a hole on the top and a bucket inside. He wiped the royal bottom with thick cloth, and inspected what was in the bucket. The groom used his observations to consult with royal doctors about the king's health. Groom of the stole was a horrible but important job, and only the most trusted servants were allowed such close contact with the king.

By the late Renaissance, close stools in wealthy homes were highly decorative items.

Head of the Bedchamber

The groom of the stole was the head of the royal bedchamber. Grooms were often given a key to the room and had to regulate access to the bedchamber and closet, even when the king was absent. The job did have some advantages, however. The groom of the stole could have the king's old clothes and old bedchamber furnishings when he had finished with them—including the royal deathbed!

King Henry VIII of England was a fearsome ruler. Imagine having to wipe his bottom!

THE HORRIBLE TRUTH

Toilet paper had been invented before the Renaissance, but few people used it in Europe to keep themselves clean. Some people used their hands, or a handful of straw. Others used strips of old cloth, which they washed and used again.

Evil Executioners

One of the nastiest jobs in Renaissance times was that of public executioner. When a court found a person guilty of committing a crime, the deadly executioner had to kill him or her in front of a crowd.

Hangings and Beheadings

Criminal acts ranged from being found to be a witch, killing someone, or plotting to overthrow a ruler. It was the gruesome job of the executioner to kill. They usually hanged or beheaded their victims. Executioners sometimes had to cook the heads and stick them on poles for all to see! Apart from their horrible duties, executioners also faced being harmed by the families of those they killed, so they often wore hoods to hide their identity while executing.

People were hanged on public gallows such as this one.

12

Other Punishments

In Renaissance times, punishments were tough, even for minor crimes. If people were caught stealing, they were locked in wooden stocks in a public square. People shouted at them and threw garbage at them! If a person told lies, he or she was forced to wear a metal head brace that stopped the tongue from moving, so the person could not speak.

THE HORRIBLE TRUTH

The phrase "money for old rope" means money earned easily, or with little effort. Some people say it comes from the Renaissance practice of cutting rope used for hangings into pieces and selling them to people as good luck charms!

Stocks were designed to humiliate people rather than hurt them.

Dung Collectors

In Renaissance cities, people couldn't flush the toilet as we do today. Human waste often collected in tanks, called cesspits, under toilets. When waste builds up, it stinks and attracts flies and other animals that can spread disease. The poor people who dealt with the stinking problem of full cesspits were gong farmers.

Gong famers had one of the smelliest jobs in the Renaissance.

A Smelly Job

Gong farmers worked at night when other city residents were asleep and it was cooler, so the waste smelled less! They shoveled the waste into buckets and emptied it into vats on horsedrawn carts. Gong farmers transported the waste into the countryside, to put on farm fields. These stinky workers always smelled pretty bad, so they were allowed to live only in particular parts of town.

Women often carried pomander balls. The balls' sweet-smelling spices and herbs disguised the women's true, stinky smell!

Rare Baths

Many people in Renaissance times were quite smelly—baths were a rare event for both rich and poor people. That's because many believed water carried diseases that entered the body through the skin. They believed that the dirt on their skin protected them. Some people masked the smell by carrying pomanders, which were metal balls that contained spices or herbs.

THE HORRIBLE TRUTH

In medieval times, one-third of Europe's population died from the Black Death, or bubonic plague. This terrible illness caused fever and the painful swelling of glands. The highly infectious disease spread fastest in cities, where people lived close to one another. In Renaissance times, there were also outbreaks of plague. In 1563, the disease killed about one-fifth of London's population.

Streets in some cities had open sewers during the Renaissance. Shown here is one such street in Croatia.

Chapter Two
Trades and Crafts

In Renaissance times, there were lots of guilds, or associations of people who did the same job. In a guild, members agreed on rules about the quality of their work and what they should charge for it.

Like most other tradespeople of the time, butchers belonged to guilds.

Guilds for Trades

The most important guilds were for jobs such as judges, wool merchants, artists, and physicians. Others were craft guilds that represented a variety of trades, from butchers to cobblers. Richer guilds used the money from the fees their members paid to help the poor and needy, and to build guildhalls where they could have meetings. They also took an active role in governing cities. Through guilds, people with trades came to be respected members of Renaissance society.

Starting at the Bottom

To join a guild, a boy had to learn a trade as an apprentice. He was rarely allowed to choose the trade—his parents chose, instead. Even if his parents had a trade, the boy could not learn from them. Apprentices sometimes had to leave home as young as 9 years old, to live with another guild member or master. Apprentices worked for free while they learned a trade, and could be harshly treated if they made mistakes. After several years, the apprentice might then, in the case of a skilled craft such as printing, produce a "masterpiece" to prove their ability. Only then could they enter the guild.

Guilds often met at grand town halls, like this one in Luebeck, Germany.

Cost of Living

People could usually earn more money in Renaissance times if they had a skilled job. These are some typical yearly wages:

merchant $200

skilled worker $20

unskilled worker $8

servant $1 to $2 (plus food and lodging)

In Renaissance times, $1 was worth around $400 in today's money, and goods were much cheaper to buy. You could buy more than 200 chickens for just $1!

17

Bloodletting Doctors

If people were sick in Renaissance times, it was the job of the doctor to try to make them better. However, a doctor's visit in Renaissance times was very different from one today!

Balancing Fluids

The doctor might start with bloodletting. This meant cutting into the patient to drain some blood into a metal cup! To treat an illness of the head, the doctor might let blood from the forehead. To treat an illness of the stomach, blood was let from the bottom. Bloodletting was based on Roman ideas about medicine. Galen was a Roman doctor who thought that people remained healthy if their body contained blood, phlegm, and stomach fluids in balanced amounts. If a person was sick, Galen's cure was to remove some of his or her body fluids to rebalance the body.

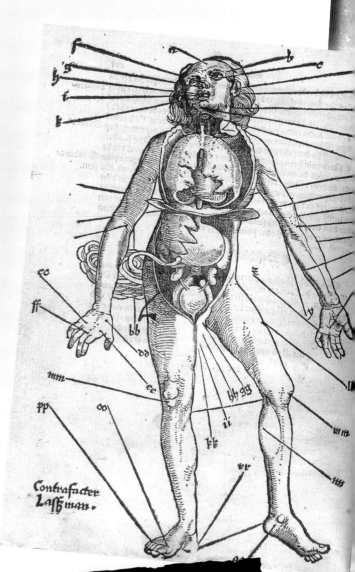

Renaissance surgery books described bloodletting points on the body.

This Renaissance doctor is giving an anatomy lesson.

New Medicine

Renaissance medicine gradually changed. Doctors began to study dead bodies and discovered new things about human anatomy. They learned how diseases spread and the importance of exercise and a healthy diet. Renaissance surgeons began to use new techniques, too. They stopped pain using drugs, and stopped bleeding by tying blood vessels. These new methods were a great step forward—in medieval times, to stop bleeding physicans burned the wound with a red-hot poker or boiling-hot oil!

THE HORRIBLE TRUTH

Did you know that the average age a person lived to in the Renaissance was 30 to 40 years old? That's around half the age that most people live to today. Many people died of common infections and diseases. The oldest and youngest were most vulnerable. One in five Renaissance babies died when they were still infants.

Artists' Assistants

A Renaissance artist's apprentice faced many hazards during their job as assistant to their master. Some poor assistants even died while helping their master work!

Preparing Paint

One of the jobs of an assistant was to prepare paints. The assistant ground up colorful rocks to make pigments, which gave the paint its color. Some of the rocks were poisonous. For example, a rock called orpiment was used to create a golden yellow pigment, but it contained the deadly chemical arsenic. If any arsenic touched the assistant's mouth, they died! It took a long time to grind orpiment into a pigment, so the assistant was in contact with the poison for days.

Being an artist's apprentice was dangerous work.

An artist's assistant ground rocks with a mortar and pestle to create the pigments his master needed.

Tough Work

Apprentices had to do other jobs, too. They made brushes by tying bunches of animal hair onto sticks. Apprentices boiled animal skins to make glue, to put on canvas to stop paint soaking through. If the apprentice's master was a sculptor, he had to carry and move huge pieces of stone. Some helped pour red-hot bronze metal into molds, to cast statues. They also had to clean and tidy the studio. Other jobs were even more unpleasant, such as cutting up a dead body so the artist could examine and better understand the human anatomy.

Value of Art

In Renaissance times, art created by a master artist was highly valued. For example, it cost around 30 florins (around $4,500) for a large wall painting. It cost much more for the best. Michelangelo was the richest Renaissance artist because he was probably the best. He earned the equivalent of $60,000 for his colossal statue, *David*. Today, this is still one of the most famous sculptures in the world.

Michelangelo learned to make sculptures, such as this one, as an apprentice.

Painful Pinners

In Renaissance times, pins were handmade and in high demand. The seams of the fancy clothing of the times were not sewn together. Instead, pins held the seams together and without them, clothes would have fallen apart! Pins were not cheap to buy, and were sometimes even given as presents. Pinners had the job of making pins.

The Pin Process

Pinners took a short length of metal wire and filed the tip to a sharp point. Then, they added a pin head, either by crimping (pinching it) or by soldering (gluing it with melted lead), to the wire. Often, the whole pin was dipped in melted tin, to make it shiny and smooth, and easier to pass through fabric.

Elaborate Renaissance clothing, like this outfit, was held together by hundreds of pins.

Child Labor

Making pins was delicate work that required nimble fingers and sharp eyes, especially in the darkness of the average Renaissance room. This meant many pinners were often children. Pinners regularly got sick from breathing in the fumes created by soldering and dipping pins in tin. Pinners struggled to get rich from their work—they were paid just $1 to make 20,000 pins!

Actors' elaborate costumes were held together by sharp pins.

Pinned On

The only actors on Renaissance stages were men, because acting was thought to be inappropriate for women. Men dressed as women to play female parts in plays. This meant wearing uncomfortable corsets and dresses, which were pinned onto the wearer in a hurry during scene changes. When it was time for a costume change, actors were often pricked over and over with sharp pins—ouch!

23

Candle Makers

Only very rich people could afford glass windows in their homes during the Renaissance, so most homes were pretty dark, even in the daytime. Electricity had not yet been invented, so it was hard for people to see at night unless they were in a room with a fire. Candles were the usual source of light, and these were made by candle makers.

Smelly Work

Candle makers usually smelled of animal fat. That's because they went from home to home to buy and collect animal fat waste, or tallow, from cooking. They melted the tallow and dipped a string in it, to cover the string in a layer of fat. The candle makers repeated this process many times, so the layers of fat built up around the string, making a candle.

Candlemaking was a long, slow, and tedious process.

Tallow and Beeswax

Tallow candles gave off weak light and smoke when they burned, but at least they were cheap. Much brighter candles could be made from beeswax, but this was too expensive for most people to buy. Beeswax candles were used in churches and in noblemen's homes. The poorest people made their own short-lived candles by dipping river plants called rushes into what little tallow they could collect from their cooking.

In the Renaissance, bees were kept to produce honey and beeswax for candles.

Beekeeping

In Renaissance times, sugar from sugarcane was discovered as a sweetener. Honey was also popular to sweeten food, to make a honey drink called mead, and the wax was also used to make candles. Many country houses and monasteries kept their own bee hives for a supply of honey and wax. The hives were made from tightly wound straw.

Chapter Three
Country Life

The great art and buildings of the renaissance, the changes to society and personal wealth all happened mostly in cities. Many of these, such as Venice, had become important as coastal trading ports. The majority of people, however, lived in the countryside in simple homes. They worked hard to grow and raise the food they needed for themselves, and for rich landlords.

The city of Venice became rich on foreign trade.

Expanding Cities

As cities grew, so did the demand for goods from the countryside. More of the food and other farm products went to the cities. New farming ideas were developed during the Renaissance, such as irrigation, which helped farmers produce more food. However, in some areas there was still not enough food to go around.

Busy Housewife

One of the toughest jobs in the Renaissance was also one of the most common, a housewife. Housewives collected firewood, baked bread, brewed beer, grew crops in the yard, milked animals, made cheese, and preserved food for times when less grew in the fields. They collected and spun wool and linen, spun cloth, and made and washed clothes. They also sold any spare produce at the market and cared for children until they were old enough to help out at home.

Crops

Different farm crops grew better in different areas because of the weather. Farmers grew many tried and trusted crops, ranging from grains, such as wheat and rice, to vegetables, including peas, carrots, and cabbage. Farmers also grew new foods that had been brought back by traders from the Americas and Asia, including beans, sweet potatoes, and squashes.

Woad Dyers

The job of the woad dyer might have been the smelliest of all Renaissance jobs. The leaves from the woad plant can be made into a strong blue dye to color cloth. In the Renaissance, the color was very popular, but the smell was not!

A Stinky Process

First, woad dyers packed crushed woad leaves into barrels and let them rot. The smell grew. Then, the dyers cooked the rotted woad with wood ash and urine for three days, to make a greenish soup. The scent was appalling. Some have described it as rotten cabbage mixed with sewage! When the mixture was ready to use, dyers dipped the cloth into it. The cloth turned green at first, but when lifted from the mixture and into the air, it turned blue.

Poor woad dyers were often outcasts because of the stench that stayed on them.

Woad was used to dye wool for tapestries.

Royal Visits

Woad production was very smelly. Queen Elizabeth I insisted that woad dyers did not make up any new batches of dye whenever she was traveling through a town. It was an unpopular trade that was usually kept within the family. You could spot a woad dyer easily, because their hands were blue and they were very smelly!

End of the Woad

Woad dyers' jobs came under threat in the sixteenth century because of a new discovery, a dye called indigo. This was made from an Asian plant that was brought to Europe from India by traders. A group of woad producers, called the woadites, tried to protect their jobs by banning indigo. However, imported indigo soon replaced woad because it had the same strong blue color, but not the terrible smell.

Charcoal Makers

Making charcoal was one of the messiest jobs of the Renaissance. However, charcoal was in huge demand. It gave off more heat than firewood, so it was a valuable fuel not only for home fires, but also for people that needed a lot of heat to do their jobs, such as glassmakers. Charcoal was also used to make gunpowder.

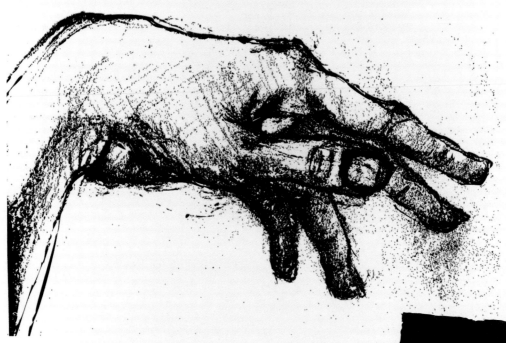

Making a Kiln

Charcoal makers collected and tightly stacked tons of fresh wood in a shallow pit. They covered the pit with damp earth and turf to make a kiln, and put some white-hot embers inside. Then, the charcoal makers left the wood to bake and smolder for up to 5 days.

Charcoal was used by Renaissance artists to create their masterpieces.

Injury of the Vert

In Renaissance times, some areas of woodland were public, and people were free to collect wood. Others were owned by kings and queens, and were places where the deer the monarchs liked to hunt lived. People who trespassed and cut branches or trees without permission on this land were fined. This crime was called injury of the vert (trees). In medieval times, it was an extremely serious offense for which you might even be blinded!

People still make charcoal today. These charcoal-making kilns are waiting to be lit.

Up in Smoke

Charcoal makers' eyes streamed from the kiln smoke. Their faces were also burned, because they constantly peered, day and night, through holes in the kiln to check that the wood was not actually burning. If the charcoal makers did not adjust the kilns, by opening or closing holes to let in more or less air, the wood might burn completely—and they would earn nothing.

Ditchdiggers

Imagine digging holes all day every day. That was the job of a ditchdigger. In Renaissance times, ditchdiggers were in demand to make hedges.

Greedy Landowners

In some areas, landowners realized they could make more money if they kept livestock, such as sheep, rather than growing crops. Around some villages, areas of shared or common land were divided into small pieces on which poor people could graze their animals. However, rather than share it, landowners used their power to take common land and keep it just for their livestock, by surrounding it with hedges. This kept other people and animals off the land.

A ditchdigger's job was dirty, damp, and boring.

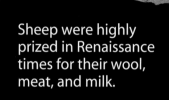

Sheep were highly prized in Renaissance times for their wool, meat, and milk.

Sheep Power!

A herd of cows was uncommon on a Renaissance farm in Europe. Many farmers instead kept sheep. Sheep were smaller, cheaper to buy, and easier to rear. They produced not only valuable wool, but also milk for drinking and making cheese, mutton, not to mention useful tallow, too. Cattle were usually kept as working animals, to pull plows.

Dig, Dig, Dig!

Ditchdiggers constantly ached and had blistered hands. To prepare the ground for a hedge, diggers used shovels and pickaxes to dig trenches several feet deep and, sometimes, hundreds of feet long. Then they piled the soil and rocks into long, neat mounds. Ditchdiggers planted hedging plants, including thorny hawthorn, on the mounds. The plants grew tightly together, creating a living fence that prevented animals, and people, from passing through.

Warreners and Fowlers

Many poor people in the Renaissance countryside ate wild food from the hedgerows, rivers, coasts, and woods, not just the food produced on farms. These wild foods included hazelnuts, eels, oysters, and badgers. Wild rabbits were not especially common, but rabbit meat and soft fur were in demand. It was the job of rabbit farmers, called warreners, to make sure there was a constant supply of rabbits, bred for their meat and fur.

In the Renaissance, rabbits were bred for their meat and fur.

Rabbits for the Poor

Warreners dug burrows for the rabbits to live in on an area of land. They guarded and surrounded the burrows with stone walls, to stop the rabbits escaping and foxes getting in. The horrid part of their job was killing the rabbits. The warreners often used ferrets to chase the rabbits out of the warren into nets. Then they killed them with a blow to the head or a twist of the neck. By the late Renaissance, warreners supplied so many rabbits that even poor people could afford to buy one for a special occasion.

Fowl Business

Fowlers supplied the ducks, swans, herons, and other water birds that were popular on Renaissance tables. Fowlers lived near lakes, rivers, and marshes, where the birds lived. Fowlers often shot their prey, but, sometimes, they used trained birds of prey to kill them.

A fowler supplied wealthy people with birds such as herons, swans, and ducks.

Freshly killed animals were stored and prepared in Renaissance kitchens.

House Bunnies

Rabbits first became house pets in Renaissance times, but only for the very rich. Most people kept animals because they were useful, or because they provided meat. Pet rabbits were pampered by their owners, and some even wrote poems about their pets when they died!

35

Chapter Four Exploring the World

Sir Francis Drake, Vasco da Gama, and Christopher Columbus were all famous Renaissance explorers. It was during the Renaissance that Europeans first sailed all the way across the world's oceans. They achieved this partly because of new technology.

New Technology

Shipbuilders had developed ships with large sails and keels. This meant the ships could go faster and move in straighter lines. Traveling on the ocean was speedier than over land, where there were few roads. Ships could also carry heavier loads than land transport, such as horse and cart. However, ocean voyage was far from easy. Sailors had lots of nasty jobs to do onboard ships, from scrubbing decks to pumping out water from the hold. They also faced many hazards, such as whippings for not following ship rules and even attacks by pirates!

Renaissance ships took explorers such as Sir Francis Drake to unexplored lands.

Perilous Pilot

The pilot of a ship was its navigator. It was an important job, but also a horrible one. If you took the wrong course, you might direct the ship onto rocks or sharp coral reefs, and sink the ship. Navigating involved a lot of guesswork. Maps of oceans were not very detailed and compasses gave users only a rough idea of direction. Pilots used the position of stars at night to figure out where they were, or looked at the water. Floating wood and seabirds usually indicated land was near.

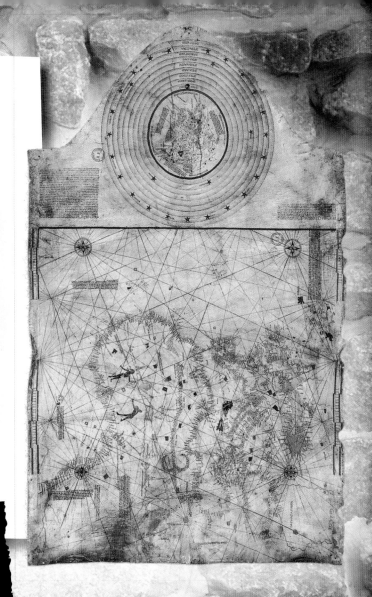

Renaissance maps were far less accurate than maps of today.

Sea Sickness

Food onboard a long Renaissance voyage was not good for a sailor's health. The only foods he had to eat were easily transported items such as salted beef, dried cheese, and hard ship's biscuits. Many sailors had bleeding gums and their teeth fell out. These were signs of a disease called scurvy. The disease is caused by not eating enough vitamin C, which is found in fresh foods, such as fruit and vegetables.

Ship's biscuits were incredibly hard— biting one could loosen a tooth!

Cabin Boys

Cabin boys or pages had a range of different jobs to do on a Renaissance ship. The poorest cabin boys had the very worst jobs to do.

Chasing Rats

Cabin boys worked in the galley, or kitchen, helping the ship's cook. They also carried food up from the hold, to the crew above. It was the job of cabin boys to chase off any rats and cockroaches that tried to enter the food stores. Sometimes, they were made to empty the officers' chamber pots. They had to climb the ship's rigging, too. They then had to crawl along the wooden spars to unfurl the sails. One slip, and they might fall to their doom.

Killing cockroaches was part of daily life for cabin boys.

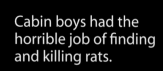

Cabin boys had the horrible job of finding and killing rats.

Sleepless Nights

Unless they were the captain or a senior member of the crew, Renaissance sailors had no cabin to sleep in. Some had no choice but to try to get a few minutes' sleep on a coil of rope or in a quiet corner. The luckier ones slept in hammocks that hung in the sheltered, but cramped, spaces inside the ship. Hammocks were discovered by Columbus in the Americas. Even in hammocks, sailors never got a full night's sleep—they had to take turns to keep watch for hazards at sea, all through the night.

Hammocks were just one of the many discoveries Columbus made in the Americas.

Rich Cabin Boys

Cabin boys from richer families who knew the officers had an easier time on a ship. They might then become an assistant to the captain. Their tasks included keeping the ship's charts in order or turning the sand clock, a device used to tell the time before clocks were invented. Knowing the time was essential when navigating a ship's course across the oceans.

The Punisher

On Renaissance ships, the crew assembled on deck two or three times a week and officers reminded them of ship rules and regulations. It was the horrible job of the ship punisher to discipline crew members.

A Feared Man

At the on-deck meeting, crew members listened to a list of jobs that had to be completed. They were also read a list of punishments they could expect if they broke the laws, worked too slowly, or did not follow orders. The most feared man onboard was the one who carried out the harsh punishments, often the quartermaster or bosun. Some of the things he had to do were pretty gruesome!

No Renaissance ship set sail without its crew being made aware of the essential rules onboard.

Terrible Punishments

Some of the horrible punishments the punisher had to carry out were:

CRIME	PUNISHMENT
swearing	Put a long, sharp pin in the sailor's mouth and clamp it closed, so his mouth bled.
slow work or minor theft	Flog the sailor with a whip called the cat-o'-nine-tails.
threatening with a knife	Cut off the sailor's hand.
stealing repeatedly	Cut off the sailor's hair, pour boiling tar onto his head, and then cover the tar with feathers.
murder	Tie the sailor to the man he had killed, and throw both the body and the sailor overboard.

A sailor would lose his hand if he threatened another sailor with a knife.

THE HORRIBLE TRUTH

The cat-o'-nine-tails was a whip used on ships. It was made of long strands of sharp, knotted leather that cut open skin. Sailors were sometimes tied to the rigging or to the ships' wheel to be whipped, and other sailors were ordered to watch. The bosun then whipped the offender a few or tens of times, depending on his crime. Once the whipping was over, a bucket of seawater was poured on the sailor to wash away the blood.

A lashing with the cat-o'-nine-tails was very painful.

Bilge Boys

In Renaissance times, ships were made of long planks of wood that were nailed together and often coated in tar. Water seeped through tiny gaps between the planks and sloshed around in the bottom, or bilge, of a ship. If enough water seeped in, it might eventually sink the ship. The sailors with the horrible job of clearing water from the bilges were called bilge boys.

Water Pumps

Bilge boys sometimes used buckets to collect water from the bilge, but more often they used different types of pumps. Some were made of a hollow log. Inside the hollow was a plunging stick, connected to a leather disk. The action of lifting the stick sucked up water. In the damp bilge, bilge boys pumped water in this way for hours on end.

Bilge water contained many horrible things, including toilet waste and rats!

Foul Water

Bilge water was not clean seawater. It contained dirty water washed down from the deck, waste from buckets used as toilets, vomit, waste food, and even dead rats. This vile soup got so smelly that sailors would faint in the stench.

Lots of mopped deck water seeped into the bilge water at the bottom of the ship.

Nº 1
CABIN - BOY.

Sea Shanties

Sea shanties were work songs sung or chanted by sailors in Renaissance times. The songs have been popular ever since. Shanties had rhythms that helped the sailors work in time with each other when carrying out different jobs. Pumping shanties helped sailors ease the boredom of pumping the bilges, and halyard shanties helped sailors pull on ropes to raise the heavy mainsails of the ship.

The End of the Renaissance

The Renaissance lasted for around 200 years, until the mid to late sixteenth century. In the late sixteenth century, huge changes took place across Europe. The biggest was that many people changed their religious beliefs. Some joined a new Protestant Christian faith brought about by Martin Luther, a German monk. Luther wanted to reduce the power of the Catholic church, which he believed to be corrupt.

Galileo Galilei shows the ruler of Venice how to use his new telescope invention.

A New Invention

Toward the end of the Renaissance, scientific discoveries made some people question religion altogether. Using a new invention called the telescope, scientists began to study the stars. They discovered that Earth moved around the sun, and therefore was not at the center of the universe. This made some people question how the world was created. Religious differences between mainly Protestant countries, such as Germany, and Catholic ones, such as Spain and Italy, even contributed to wars.

Catastrophes

For some people, the end of the Renaissance was marked by other horrible events. In London, in the middle of the seventeenth century, the Great Plague took hold. Around 100,000 people died from bubonic plague. Then, less than 20 years later, a terrible fire called The Great Fire of London swept through the city, destroying thousands of buildings.

The Great Fire of London devastated England's capital city in 1666.

Life After the Renaissance

After Renaissance artists such as Leonardo da Vinci died, new artists emerged. New artists who became popular, such as Caravaggio, painted dramatic images. These artists used light and shade to show great emotion and powerful ideas. There were also many new inventions, such as newspapers and submarines, and discoveries, such as the continent of Australia. However, at the end of the Renaissance, daily life for most people did not change greatly. There were still horrible jobs to do, including emptying the bilges, collecting dung, and dyeing cloth.

Caravaggio's portraits showed more emotion than those of the Renaissance period.

Glossary

anatomy the study of the structure and parts that make up the human body

apprentice a person who learns a trade while working for an employer for low or no wages

bilge the lowest compartment on a ship where the two sides of the ship meet

bosun an officer in charge of the supervision and maintenance of a ship and its equipment

bubonic plague a bacterial disease that can be transmitted by flea bites to rodents and humans

cesspits pits for storing sewage and, sometimes, other waste

culture the customs, arts, values, and achievements of a particular nation or group of people

embers the hot, glowing piece of wood, charcoal, or coal left in a dying fire

exported goods or services sent and sold to other countries

governing ruling

gruel thin liquid food of oatmeal, or other similar food, boiled in milk or water

guilds associations of craftspeople who share the same job

imported goods and services brought from other countries

irrigation watering plants and crops

keels beams that run along the bottom a ship, from front to back

landlords people who own and rent land or buildings to others

navigator a person who guides or directs the route or course of a ship or other vehicle

perspective how things look relative to one another as determined by their distance from the viewer

poisonous a substance that makes a living thing very sick or kills them

polluted made dirty or poisonous

pomanders hollow balls with herbs and sweet-smelling things in them

scurvy a disease caused by a lack of vitamin C

sewage human waste that is today carried away in sewers and drains

tallow the fat of sheep or oxen, used for making candles or soap

taxes money people have to pay to governments (or rulers) that should be used to provide public goods and services

trespassed entered someone else's property without permission

urine liquid waste from the body

warren a network of connected rabbit burrows under the ground

For More Information

Books

Hinds, Kathryn. *Everyday Life in the Renaissance*. New York, NY: Marshall Cavendish Benchmark, 2010.

Huntley, Theresa. *Women in the Renaissance*. New York, NY: Crabtree Publishing, 2010.

Romanek, Trudee. *Great Ideas of the Renaissance*. New York, NY: Crabtree Publishing, 2010.

Websites

Learn more about the great Renaissance artist and inventor Leonardo da Vinci at this website:
www.ducksters.com/biography/leonardo_da_vinci.php

Meet some Renaissance explorers, scientists, and other personalities on this wonderful website:
www.yesnet.yk.ca/schools/projects/renaissance

If you would like to try spice trading and exploring in Renaissance times, check out the interactive activity on this website:
www.learner.org/interactives/renaissance/spicetrade

Index